RENEWING YOUR MIND

THE KEY TO UNDENIABLE SUCCESS

2ND EDITION

RENEWING YOUR MIND

THE KEY TO UNDENIABLE SUCCESS

2ND EDITION

Henry T. Wells

KINGDOM RULE
PUBLISHING
WWW.KINGDOMRULE.COM

A division of Consuming Fire Incorporated
WWW.CONSUMINGFIREINC.COM

HAMPTON, VIRGINIA

This publication is designed to provide competent and reliable information regarding the subject matter covered. However, it is sold with the understanding that the author and publisher are not engaged in rendering legal, financial or other professional advice. The author and publisher specifically disclaim any liability that is incurred from the use or application of the contents of this book.

All scripture references (unless noted) are taken from the King James Version of the Bible.

Merriam-Webster definitions are taken from www.merriam-webster.com

Published by Kingdom Rule Publishing, a subsidiary of Consuming Fire Incorporated.

Copyright © 2008 by Henry T. Wells.
All Rights Reserved.

Kingdom Rule Nonfiction
Kingdom Rule Publishing

Kingdom Rule Publishing
206 W Taylor Ave, Hampton, VA 23663

Kingdom Rule Publishing is a subsidiary of Consuming Fire Incorporated
Visit our website at www.consumingfireinc.com.

Printed in the United States of America

First Kingdom Rule Publishing Printing: September 2008
Second Kingdom Rule Publishing Printing: November 2010
ISBN: 978-0-9802460-1-8

Cover design by Stephen Blackmon.

Dedication

I dedicate this book to my darling wife and friend of 18 years, Donyale. You are the wind beneath my wings. Thanks for putting up with me so long. I am eternally grateful to you for your undying love and support.

Contents

Introduction: The Assignment..........11

1. Regional Mindsets 17

2. The Formation of Our Thought Life..........23

3. Developing the Mind of Christ..........31

4. Changing Your Mind..........43

5. Transformed by the Word..........51

6. The Subconscious..........57

7. Steps for Change..........65

8. The Results of Renewing Your Mind..........75

Introduction
THE ASSIGNMENT

At the time of this writing, I have been a pastor for just over five years in the beautiful city of Williamsburg, Virginia. I can truly say it has been a challenging, yet rewarding adventure. One of the greatest challenges I found was the search for my specific assignment to the city of Williamsburg; the particular thing(s) that God called me here to do. Every church occupies a niche in the kingdom-- a specific call that answers a need within the Body of Christ. I must admit that I really didn't know much about that or the city when I received my assignment here in 2005. However this time of seeking God, researching, watching and praying has turned out to be one of the most rewarding periods of my life. I have begun to understand some of the intricacies of our assignment since saying yes to God and walking into this unique yet universal mission field.

Williamsburg, Virginia, in some regards, is a literal step back in time. It is a place where tourists gather each year and marvel at its historical significance. It was actually the first capitol city of the New World. Many Civil War battles were fought near it and its neighboring communities Jamestown and Yorktown. Williamsburg is the very fabric in the tapestry that makes up American history. I consider myself fortunate to live in a city with such a rich history. On the other hand, this area also has an unfortunate bit of history that I am not proud of.

For while the legal institution of slavery ceased, the mental mindset of slavery is alive and well.

Williamsburg is the birthplace of slavery in the United States. Africans arrived in Jamestown in 1619 as indentured servants. But by 1680, things changed. What followed is nearly 200 years of enforced servitude of Africans and their descendents and the proliferation of racially based slavery. In 1863, the Emancipation Proclamation became law and forever ended the legal institution of slavery.

INTRODUCTION: THE ASSIGNMENT

What is remarkable is that, nearly one hundred fifty years later, slavery still exists. There are fourth and fifth generation citizens who remain in bondage. For while the legal institution of slavery ceased, the mental mindset of slavery is alive and well.

Years ago the Lord began dealing with me about the importance and power of mindsets. Wikipedia defines a mindset like this:

> "**Mindset** - ... a set of assumptions, methods or notations held by one or more people or groups of people which is so established that it creates a powerful incentive within these people or groups to continue to adopt or accept prior behaviors, choices or tools. This phenomenon of cognitive bias is also sometimes described as *mental inertia*, "groupthink" or a "paradigm", and it is often difficult to counteract its effects upon analysis and decision making processes."

A mindset is simply a set mind. It is a predilection to respond predictably. Knowing about your or another person's mindset helps to understand and predict behavior. Your mindset predetermines your perception and responses to a situation.

In general, our mindsets determine how we view the world, what we believe and how we behave. Behavior, habits, discipline, be they good or bad, begin with our mindset. Our mindsets can dictate aspects of our spiritual life as well. Whether we view God as an all-powerful, vengeful deity or as a close intimate friend is often the result of our mindset.

INTRODUCTION: **THE ASSIGNMENT**

— *Food for Thought* —

1. Do you know your specific assignment within the Body of Christ, (what God has called you here to do)?

2. Could there be mindsets that are making it more difficult for you to accomplish that assignment?

Chapter One
REGIONAL MINDSETS

What has been revealed to me is that just as individual mindsets determine how a person thinks, there is a wholistic perspective as well. There are group mindsets. There are specific regions in the world in which certain mindsets prevail. The last few elections show this. Politicians have caught on. They have designated that there are "red states" and "blue states." One is deemed more conservative and one more liberal. Wisely, those running for office have begun to target their campaign efforts based on this colorful designation. Consider San Francisco or Las Vegas. While every resident doesn't think the exact same way, there is a general tendency to be more accepting of alternative lifestyles and liberal political views there.

The spiritual climate that is established in a region is a persistent phenomenon. Just as the issues of racism or sexism in this country did not evaporate the moment minorities or women received the legal right to vote, many spiritual issues still remain and need to be dealt with even after the fear of incarceration or retribution causes people to stop acting on their mindset of superiority. These twisted mindsets are now active in more subtle forms because laws don't support the activity in its more obvious means of manifestation.

While the Emancipation Proclamation ended the legal and physical system of slavery, the slavery mindset remains. I personally know individuals in their forties who have never been more than 50 miles outside of Williamsburg. Their exposure is limited; therefore their outlook on life is limited. Consequently, their mindsets are perpetuated regardless of the advancements being made throughout the country in either spiritual or social realms. Unless we make a direct, purposeful and deliberate change, they will continue to persist.

A slavery mindset can be considered as a fixed system of thinking. The peculiar institution of slavery forced a caste system of the haves and

CHAPTER ONE: REGIONAL MINDSETS

always will have to the don't haves and won't ever haves. It caused a sense of superiority (for the owners) and inferiority (of the owned). Slavery required a learned helplessness or passivity of the bondsmen. With the threat of separation from family friends and home ever looming, a slave's existence and security relied solely on the benevolence of a 'master'. The slavery mindset is one of poverty, low self-esteem, passivity, and helplessness.

> *Consequently, as a people, we become products of our environment and victims of spiritual climates that existed long before we were exposed to them.*

We have other problems in our city that stem from other mindsets such as cyclic drug addiction, incest, sex crimes, violence, poverty etc. However, Williamsburg is not the only case where there are prevailing negative mindsets. Throughout this country there are ghettos where drug dealers are glorified, pimps are praised and crime is not criminal in the eyes of far too many of its citizens. It's the norm. Consequently, as a people, we become products of our environment and victims of spiritual climates that existed long before we were exposed to them.

My motivation for writing this book is to help people identify unhealthy mindsets and systems of thinking that keep us oppressed and unproductive in the kingdom of God. My aim is to equip believers with practical biblical tools that will help facilitate change in our modes of thinking and therefore change in our behavior that result in reaching higher and becoming all that God has designed for us to be.

CHAPTER ONE: **REGIONAL MINDSETS**

— *Food for Thought* —

1. Have you seen the mindset of anyone close to you change over time? (For example: has someone you've known developed a different disposition toward women, or men, or people of another race, or one's health, or war?)

2. Have you noticed any of your own mindsets change recently?

3. What behaviors and/or attitudes changed along with that change in mindset?

Chapter Two
THE FORMATION OF OUR THOUGHT LIFE

"I beseech you therefore, brethren, by the mercies of God that you present your bodies a living sacrifice, holy, acceptable unto God, which is your reasonable service. *And be not conformed to this **world**, but be ye transformed by the renewing of your mind*, that you may prove what is that good and acceptable and perfect will of God."

— Romans 12:1-2

The bible directs us not to be conformed or shaped according to the patterns of this world. But what does that mean exactly? It means that something or someone is directing your thinking. At this very moment, you are being either transformed or conformed. The system of the world is designed to form you into a replica of itself. Throughout our society we are exposed to a plethora of ideologies, perspectives and arguments that are not in agreement with the Word of God. The scriptures clearly warn us that the world has its own philosophies and views on how we should live, what we should pursue, how we should treat each other, whom we should serve and what to seek, desire, and love.

> "Love not the world neither the things of the world… for all that is in the world, the lust of the flesh, and the lust of the eye, and the pride of life, is not of the Father but of the world."
>
> — I John 2:15-16

This is an admonition to flee lusts. To flee is to run as if your life depended on it. That is how much danger there is in going with the flow of the world. The world's system of thinking is geared towards our lusts and greed. The sentiment presented through the media can be encapsulated in *if it feels good, just do it* and *anything goes as long as you don't hurt anyone*. This way of thinking is ungodly and unhealthy. This has a profound effect on our thought life.

CHAPTER TWO: THE FORMATION OF OUR THOUGHT LIFE

The conforming process is via three primary influences that shape our thinking: Heredity, Environment and Experiences.

HEREDITY

How we process information is partly due to our heredity or what has been passed down to us genetically in terms of our cognitive processes. Our intellectual capability and much of our personality are partially the result of our genetic code. For example, if one or both of our parents were analytical, then there's a great chance that we are going to be analytical. Scientific evidence bears this out. Twins that have been reared apart inexplicably have remarkably similar traits, interests, hobbies, or professions. This shows that there is a genetic influence on behavior built within the structure of our DNA.

ENVIRONMENT

Our environment plays a role in the formation of our thought life. Whether we grew up in the country or the city, whether we grew up in the hood or in the suburbs, our environment affects our perspective on life, how we process information, and respond to new situations. A person who grew in an urban environment may approach social situations with caution. He may scan and scope out a new place. Assess who's who and decide if it is safe. Someone who lives in a smaller town may not display the same level of caution. They may not even consider the possibility of danger in the same social setting. Your environment has a very profound effect on how you think.

EXPERIENCES

Much of who we are stems from our experiences. This ranges from that which we've gained from school and organized education to the things we've learned from life; the things we've been through; if we've been hurt; if we've been abused; if we've been mistreated; if someone has treated us well. All of these experiences affect our system of thinking. Whether your experiences were good or bad, they had an effect on how you think today. Those experiences make up the canvas of your mind that is painted on your subconscious. They affect how you operate in this life.

"For my thoughts are not your thoughts

CHAPTER TWO: THE FORMATION OF OUR THOUGHT LIFE

neither are your ways my ways, saith the Lord. For as the heavens are higher than the earth, so are my ways higher than your ways and my thoughts than your thoughts."
— Isaiah 55:8,9

Left to ourselves, we don't think like God and His thoughts supersede our own. It's so good that it does not stop there. We have an awesome promise. He has promised to renew, wash and cleanse us so that we will begin to think in a new dimension, on a higher plane. This is not a natural thing. The thoughts of God are only ascertained through the spirit realm.

"But the natural man receiveth not the things of the Spirit of God: for they are foolishness unto him: neither can he know them, because they are spiritually discerned."
— I Corinthians 2:14

So if we would know His thoughts, we must draw nigh unto Him, we must seek to rise above the natural man and access the spirit realm. Rightly accessing the spirit realm starts with the Word of God. The Word of God is no doubt where it all begins!

CHAPTER TWO: THE FORMATION OF OUR THOUGHT LIFE

— *Food for Thought* —

1. How closely do you monitor/control your thought life? Have you ever taken the time and opportunity to invite God into your thought life? If not, do so now.

2. Think about some of the memorable experiences in your life. How have they affected or changed your system of thinking? Were those changes good? Were they inline with Scripture?

Chapter Three
DEVELOPING THE MIND OF CHRIST

It is God's desire for you to be transformed into the greatest possible version of yourself. Jeremiah 29:11 states that God has plans for us—plans for a hope, posterity, a future and an expected end. That means that when the Lord God Almighty considers us, he has destiny in mind. He knows what He created. He has seen the end from the beginning and knows our true potential and destination. And he has equipped us with all that we need to get there. This is part of why we must seek our affirmation and our sense of acceptance from Him. He knows what you can and should truly be once you shed self-imposed limitations and self-destructive thinking. When you renew your mind, you shed worldly mindsets. God wants us to think like Jesus thought; to have the mind of Christ. Only then can we fulfill reach our highest height and make reality the destiny he has for us.

"Let this mind be in you that was also in Christ Jesus."

— Philippians 2:5

Why would the Word tell us to "let" or allow the mind of Christ to be in us? Allowing the mind of Christ to be in us is not an automatic, effortless thing. We can, through our deliberate action or passivity, allow or deny the mind of Christ to be in us. God wants us to give him access to every area of our lives…including our thought life. We are not robots functioning as automatons. We have free will and free choice. We are rather like free agents.

In sports, you have signed players and free agents. Free agents are free to select the team they play on. In the kingdom of God, we are free agents. We are able to elect to choose a course of action and make a decision. Do we score points for the good guys or aid the enemy? It's up to us. The Word says to choose ye this day whom you will serve. Because face it, you are serving someone—either God or Satan.

We must, as an act of our will, renew our minds

CHAPTER THREE: DEVELOPING THE MIND OF CHRIST

and allow the mind of Christ to be in us. This is one of the biggest challenges we face. While you are on earth, there is a constant spiritual warfare for the control of our mind. We are fed a continual diet of the world's ideologies. We are bombarded by TV, radio, newspapers, commercials, advertisements, and the Internet. We are taught that if we have this car, house, vacation, or lifestyle then we will be happy. We are shown images equating wealth or decadence with popularity and joy. We must challenge the world's philosophy with the truth of God's Word.

In the kingdom of God, we are free agents. We are able to elect to choose a course of action and make a decision. Do we score points for the good guys or aid the enemy?

When we get saved, when we accept Jesus Christ's perfect gift of redemption, His presence comes into our hearts. Our spirit man is born again. From this point we have a pure and new-found connection to the Lord whereby we can commune and communicate with Him. Immediately upon salvation you are transformed in your spirit.

However, your soul and your body stay virtually the same.

We are triune beings. You are a spirit, with a soul, in a body. This is a critical understanding required in discussing your life in Christ and the process of renewing your mind.

> "And the very God of peace sanctify you wholly; and I pray God your whole **spirit** and **soul** and **body** be preserved blameless unto the coming of our Lord Jesus Christ."
> — I Thessalonians 5:23

BODY

We are all quite aware of our physical body; of its senses and sensations, its capabilities and desires. Even as a baby, we come to understand the sensation of touch or sight. We physically feel exhaustion or hunger. The body is a very effective tool for interacting in this world - for manifesting good or evil, for serving the Lord or serving our physical cravings. But we must bring our bodies under subjection if we are to please God. Scripture repeatedly reminds us not to be driven by the lusts of the body or 'the flesh.':

CHAPTER THREE: DEVELOPING THE MIND OF CHRIST

"But put ye on the Lord Jesus Christ, and make not provision for the **flesh**, to fulfill the **lusts** thereof."

— Romans 13:14
(see also Galatians 5:24, or
I Peter 2:11 or I Peter 4:2)

Our body's needs are easy to identify and difficult to ignore. The pang of hunger and the need for sleep are obvious methods the body uses to communicate. What salvation did for us is to give us the option of obeying its every whim or triumphing over it.

Just like with Adam and Eve, situations will arise wherein we have to choose whether we will obey God, or obey the desires of our physical bodies. And much like the case of Adam and Eve, the wrong decision can have serious consequences.

"Among whom also we all had our conversation in times past in the **lusts** of our **flesh**, fulfilling the desires of the **flesh** and of the mind; and were by nature the children of wrath, even as others."

— Ephesians 2:3

Your body's voice is the flesh. And flesh's longtime companion is lust. Lust wants what it wants. And it wants it NOW. The reason that that the message of the world is so effective is that it feeds the lusts of the flesh. The Bible speaks of ways to avoid the insistent demands of the flesh. Galatians 5 tells us to walk in the spirit (in that new part of us made perfect by our salvation) so that we do not walk in the flesh. We are also admonished to make NO provision for the flesh (Romans 13:14) by putting on Christ Jesus. Read this in the amplified for clarity.

> "But clothe yourself with the Lord Jesus Christ (the Messiah), and make no provision for [indulging] the flesh [put a stop to thinking about the evil cravings of your physical nature] to [gratify its] desires (lusts)."

The more you heed the voice of flesh, the louder it speaks, and the more it wants. Flesh and lust are insatiable. If you constantly satisfy its cravings, the voice of the flesh becomes more demanding and deafening and will drown out the voice of the Spirit. How do we turn the tables and drown out flesh? The way that we triumph over the flesh is by regulating our thinking. The bible tells us to think on specific things in Philippians. Thoughts that are lovely, pure and peaceable. Winning the war over flesh is mental combat.

SOUL

Though the Word is very clear about the dangers of following the lusts of the flesh, we must also be wary of the lusts of the soul. A man's soul is composed of his:

- Mind
- Will
- Emotions
- Imagination
- Intellect

The soul of man is his guiding force. Here he processes the sense information that he receives from his body. Here he also processes the spiritual information he receives through his spirit from God. A man's soul decides whom he will follow; what he will do. This is the power of the will.

The imagination and intellect also possess the opportunity to be used either by God or the flesh. The same imagination that can envision and interpret the spiritually received plan of God so that it can be communicated to other men can also be used to devise wicked and malicious inventions or plot cruelty, lasciviousness, and evil. The intellect was created to meditate upon the things of God, and seek His mysteries (Philippians 4:8 & Proverbs 25:2).

When God breathed His Spirit into the Body of Adam, Adam became a living soul. (Genesis 2:7). From this point, God decided to give Adam dominion. Adam (the soul of man) has had the power to choose ever since. This is no less true today.

"And the spirits of the prophets are subject to the prophets."
— I Corinthians 14:32

Some also refer to the soul as the personality. It encompasses how we think and feel about the situations and people we come in contact with. It contains the conscious and subconscious mind. It is the seat of both rational and irrational thought and the base of our self-awareness.

The soul has its own lusts to contend with, such as pride, jealousy, dishonesty or vain unholy imaginations. The soul is where mindsets reside; where the seeds of slavery, prejudice, arrogance and malice are planted. Here they can be uprooted or fed. They can be washed away or they can grow into a destructive force.

SPIRIT

Four of Merriam-Webster's definitions of spirit are:

1. An animating or vital principle held to give life to physical organisms.
2. The activating or essential principle influencing a person <acted in a *spirit* of helpfulness... an inclination, impulse, or tendency of a specified kind: MOOD
3. Special attitude or frame of mind... the feeling, quality, or disposition characterizing something <undertaken in a *spirit* of fun>.
4. A person having a character or disposition of a specified nature.

The biblical descriptions of spirit are not unlike Merriam-Webster's definitions. In Genesis 2 we see God breathed spirit into Adam and he became a living soul. Spirit animated him and gave him life.

In the word, we also see the term spirit used as a tendency or mood, such as in Isaiah 61:3:

> "To appoint unto them that mourn in Zion, to give unto them beauty for ashes, the oil of joy for mourning, the garment of praise for the spirit of heaviness; that they might be called trees of righteousness, the planting of the LORD, that he might be glorified."

However, the term spirit in Scripture is most often used to describe either the Holy Spirit (when used with the capital "S"), or that ethereal essence of someone that is their nature; the attributes of their driving force and deepest desires.

When Adam sinned, man died. He lost his ability to steadfastly set his deepest desires and driving force upon the things of God; upon something good outside of himself. He lost the ability to seek God and connect with Him on his own (Psalm 14:1-3). But thank God for Jesus. When we are born again, we are re-given the ability to follow and commune with God's Holy Spirit.

When we accept Christ as our personal savior our spirit is transformed and we receive new life.

CHAPTER THREE: DEVELOPING THE MIND OF CHRIST

Though we now have a spirit that has the ability to follow God, our soul must still decide to follow that spirit in order for our bodies to behave correctly. That spirit gives us the strength and guidance to pursue the desires of God. But that information must still be communicated to the soul. The decision to act on the new divine direction must still be made in the soul. From this point, the soul still has to be converted. The conversion from being ruled by the world's ideologies or flesh to appropriating the dominion you have regained over your soul is a process that requires you to deliberately purpose in your mind to change.

Chapter Four
CHANGING YOUR MIND

"Therefore, my beloved, as ye have always obeyed, not as in my presence only, but now much more in my absence, work out your own salvation with fear and trembling."
— Philippians 2:12

As we know, the perfect work of Christ was finished at the cross.

"For by grace are we saved, through faith. And that not of yourselves, it is the gift of God."
— Ephesians 2:8

The Apostle Paul was the early church's greatest advocate for the fullness of salvation being accomplished in Christ's work on the cross. He frequently contended that no amount of good works or obedience to the law could take credit for our spirit's salvation. Our hope was in faith in Christ alone. We cannot earn it. So 'working out your own salvation' as seen in Philippians cannot refer to one's spirit.

Although the Word clearly indicates that our spirit's salvation lies in faith, our success in life as one of His children lies in our ability to hear God's Word and ongoing guidance, receive it and obey. This is how we please God:

> "For if ye live after the flesh, ye shall die: but if ye through the Spirit do mortify the deeds of the body, ye shall live. For as many as are led by the Spirit of God, they are the sons of God."
> — Romans 8:14

It is also shown to apply to our tangible success:

> "This book of the law shall not depart out of thy mouth; but thou shalt meditate therein day and night, that thou mayest observe to do according to all that is written therein: for then thou shalt make thy way prosperous, and then thou shalt have good success.
> — Joshua 1:8

CHAPTER FOUR: CHANGING YOUR MIND

Interestingly, the scriptures reveal that accepting Christ into our hearts *alone* will not make us successful in life. Though God offers forgiveness and Heaven if we would just believe Him and receive His grace, that alone does not guarantee earthly success. It does not even guarantee success in our Christian walk.

Although our spirits are born anew the instant we accept Christ, our bodies and souls remain the same. They function the same. The only thing that changes is our spirit. We still have much work to do from this point. Someone may have told you that everything was going to change when you receive Christ in your heart. I was told the same thing when I received Christ. I thank God for the change in my heart and spirit that did occur. But it didn't take long to realize that I still had to deal with the same mind I had before salvation. Salvation for your spirit is instantaneous. But the saving of your soul is a process.

The soul is the compartment of the mind, will, imagination, intellect and emotions. All of these components must now be realigned with this new life in Christ. Each component of the soul affects the others. We've all seen this to be true. Each of us have had days when we started thinking negative thoughts, and it put us in a bad mood (emotion). Each of our emotions at times have been strong enough to alter what we chose to do (our will). Most of us have rationalized our way out of doing something that we knew we should do at one point or another. The same can be said for our daydreaming; what we let our fears or imagination convince us to do.

The mind is the anchor component because it tells the others how to behave. If our mind is flawed then what we produce in life will be evidence of it. Whatever our lives look like right now is a result of what we have been thinking. Your real life resembles your thought life. If we want to have a better life, we need to have better thoughts. The decision maker (your mind) must be changed if we want to see success in our Christian walk and physical life.

One of my greatest accomplishments in life has been gaining of control over my mind. The mind is a powerful tool. I say this all of the time: "You can turn a heaven into a hell or a hell into a heaven all

CHAPTER FOUR: CHANGING YOUR MIND

in your mind." You can have the best situation, but in your mind you can make it the worst situation. Things can go unchanged around you, but you can change them in your mind. Your mind can be your greatest asset or liability.

The mind's perspective carries great power. For as it controls the will, it controls the body. As it controls your body it controls your life. You can only achieve what you are able conceive in your own mind. Your limitations in life are in many ways self-imposed. They are directly connected to what you perceive in your mind.

You can turn a heaven into a hell or a hell into a heaven all in your mind.

The situations and realities of our lives are not a result of what we are thinking at any one given moment but what we think systematically. We live through our thoughts. The Word says 'as a man thinketh in his heart so is he' (Proverbs 23:7). The thoughts that are in your heart are there continually.

For example, when in church, most people think the right things because of the atmosphere and the influence of the Word of God on them for that period of time. It would be wonderful if we could stay in this frame of mind all the time, but the truth is we go back to our unstable environments and the story goes on. If we could somehow sustain the good thoughts that we have in church, then we could consistently produce pleasant things in our lives.

The fruit that is produced in a person's life is based upon his or her sustained thinking or system of thinking, meaning how we think most of the time. Ultimately, we need to cultivate healthy thoughts and a healthy mindset so that God can use us as He desires to without limitations.

Cultivating that healthy mindset and changing our system of thinking is a deliberate process. We have to be very purposeful in the course of changing it because the mind is already saturated with inferior thought patterns from the world. Our mind is shaped based on the old man; the former person / self-destructive spirit we were before we received Christ. This old man has been operating all along developing a distorted system of thinking based on our heredity, environment and experiences. This skewed system, devoid of God's truth, is how we think. This is how we initially attempt to fix any problems. This is how we approach life. But as we yield ourselves to the influence of the Word, we can and will be changed.

Chapter Five
TRANSFORMED BY THE WORD

"For the word of God is quick, and powerful, and sharper than any two edged sword, piercing even to the dividing asunder of *soul* and *spirit*, and of the joints and marrow (*body*), and is a discerner of the thoughts and intents of the heart.."

— Hebrews 4:12

Now that we know the necessity and reality of revising our system of thinking; of releasing negative mindsets and taking on positive ones, we need to see how to actually accomplish it. As with most things in life, knowing and doing are not the same. How do we avoid the trap of falling back into our old patterns of thinking? Changing our ways is at times simple, but at other times difficult. Any believer who has sought to change habits; to do right and serve God for long will tell you - the old man defends himself, vigorously. Praise be to God that we can always look to Him to provide a way of escape, a path to victory.

> "It is the spirit that quickeneth; the flesh profiteth nothing: the words that I speak unto you, they are spirit, and they are life."
>
> — John 6:63

The Word of God is our foremost weapon against the old man and his system of thinking. Until you transform your mind by the Word, it will remain the same. Ephesians 4:22 bids us "...put off, concerning your former conduct, the old man which grows corrupt according to the deceitful lusts, and *be renewed in the spirit of your mind.*"

The Word of God comes to challenge everything we know. Everyone has a philosophy for living, but when our philosophy contradicts His Truth, we as believers, and in fact all people who desire good in life, have a responsibility to dump our philosophy and receive His Truth. Your mind crosses over into your new life in Christ. Like the body, your mind does not automatically

CHAPTER FIVE: TRANSFORMED BY THE WORD

change. You have in your mind 'Before Christ' information, and you begin to gain 'After Christ' information. The 'Before Christ' information is already settled in you. The 'After Christ' information from the Word of God is what you should use to replace the 'Before Christ' information whenever they conflict.

Everyone has a philosophy for living, but when our philosophy contradicts His Truth, we as believers, and in fact all people who desire good in life, have a responsibility to dump our philosophy and receive His Truth.

"(For the weapons of our warfare are not carnal, but mighty through God to the pulling down of strong holds;) Casting down imaginations, and every high thing that exalteth itself against the knowledge of God, and bringing into captivity every thought to the obedience of Christ;"
— II Corinthians 10:4,5

So now we see that our success lies in renewing our minds. We see that the Word of God can renew our minds. But if that is all there is to it, then why aren't all believers who attend church walking in their full potential and divine success? Maybe there's more to hearing the Word than just hearing the Word.

CHAPTER FIVE: **TRANSFORMED BY THE WORD**

— Food for Thought —

1. Name at least one mindset or behavior that you want to change.

2. Find at least three scripture verses that give God's perspective on that subject? Type them or write them down on a piece of paper that you will keep.

Chapter Six
THE SUBCONSCIOUS

Every person has a subconscious. This subconscious is our autopilot. Your subconscious is what you use when you're on the road driving, talking on the cell phone and writing something down all at the same time. When you're doing all of these things at once, your subconscious is driving that car. Have you ever gone somewhere and said, "Man, I don't even remember passing exit 87?"

Your mind is designed to multitask allowing you to do things (which you've done before) whether you are focusing on them or not. Your subconscious is performing the task it has been trained to do while your focused mind works elsewhere. Likewise, when we see things recur repeatedly in our lives, it's a sign that our autopilot has been active in that area producing the results it learned to produce before.

The canvas of our minds has already been painted a certain way when we get saved. So, when we come to Christ, we already have a developed subconscious. The old man is not just your conscious memories. He is ingrained in you. When you face problems in life, the way that you handle them is actually an automatic transference from your subconscious to your conscious.

There's a reason why people have bad relationships over and over again. It's because their subconscious keeps telling them to do the same things, pick the same type of people, and act and react the same way. Therefore they keep producing bad relationships. What has been painted on the canvas of their mind has caused a negative impact to where he or she gets to a certain point in the relationship and the same things keep happening. The subconscious is running their relationship, so they keep having the same results.

Your subconscious is not going to change until you prove to it that the Word of God is reliable.

When we come to God, He challenges the

errors residing in our subconscious.

He tells us to store this 'After Christ' information in our subconscious mind. From there it can be drawn up into our conscious mind so that the new truths and 'After Christ' information will be consistently acted upon.

There are a number of situations that bypass our conscious mind and nearly force us to act from our instincts. Pressure, fear and danger are just three of the atmospheres that cause us to act directly out of our subconscious mind. Because of this, it becomes imperative that we not only hear and understand the Word with our conscious mind, but that these 'After Christ' truths rewrite our subconscious. If they do not, our thinking will never really change. We will only be able to say amen when we think something sounds good; to perpetrate or experiment with Godliness, not incorporate it into our being. The Word of God must be given access to our thinking on every level. It must be given free course to rule over our mindsets. Otherwise, we become saints with a worldly mind, having worldly issues; saints with sinner problems.

Please note that it takes more than one time hearing something to change the patterns of our subconscious. The things that you are producing in your life are not the result of what you are thinking some of the time, but what you are thinking *most* of the time.

"As a man thinketh in his heart, so is he."
— Proverbs 23:7

It's not *just* as he *thinketh*, but as he thinketh *in his heart,* because what is in your heart has been established. Those patterns were established with years of pain, misinformation, bad teaching and faulty assumptions. They're not likely to change in a day. There are reasons why the Lord told Joshua to meditate therein day and night (Joshua 1:8). David had the same revelation (Psalm 1:1,2). They sought to rewrite their subconscious. They are also two of the greatest examples of success stories we have.

"So shall my word be that goeth forth out of my mouth: it shall not return unto me void, but it shall accomplish that which I please, and it shall prosper in the thing whereto I sent it."

CHAPTER SIX: **THE SUBCONSCIOUS**

— Isaiah 55:11

When we fully realize how true, consistent, and reliable God's Word is, our subconscious mind begins to change. We develop confidence in His Word. Confidence is faith with a history. We begin to not just say that we believe God's Word but to actually KNOW that it is true. We learn that the Word is infallible…it cannot ever fail. We begin to have revelation that the Word of God is reliable. We can count on it if all else fails. The longer we are in Christ, the more he is able to change us through our system of thinking.

Your subconscious is not going to change until you prove to it that the Word of God is reliable. This is another thing that must be trained. It is trained by two intimately connected means. The first is saturating your mind with the Word.

When we finally realize how true, consistent and reliable God's Word is, our subconscious mind begins to change.

"So then faith cometh by hearing, and hearing by the Word of God."

— Romans 10:17

There are two hearings mentioned in this text. Saturating yourself in the Word in practical terms means to read the Word, hear it preached and expounded upon, to speak the Word aloud, and to rehearse it in your own voice. When you employ these multiple methods, it is like sending a barrage against anti-biblical messages. It allows you to replace your old systems of thought with the infallible Word of the Almighty God.

The second component is experiencing the One in whom you are placing your faith.

"…nevertheless I am not ashamed: for I know whom I have believed, and am persuaded that He is able to keep that which I have committed unto him against that day."
— II Timothy 1:12

The more you come to know the Word, the more you know the truth, who you were created to be and what has been promised to you. The more you come to know Him, the more you know how well-placed your faith is, who destined you for success and how able He is to help you achieve it.

It's hard to live a saved life with a worldly mind.

People struggle so badly because they are in church but they have not challenged their old man; they have not renewed their mind. They are hearing the Word, ever learning, but unable to come into the knowledge of the truth. Your subconscious will continue to act the way that it has been acting until you challenge it! People continue doing the same things that they have been doing until their minds are challenged to change.

Chapter Seven
STEPS FOR CHANGE

1. IDENTIFY THE PROBLEM

In what area of life would you like to have more success?

Take time to truly think about that question. In order to change our system of thinking, we must first recognize the need for change. We have to specify the unhealthy mindsets that interfere with kingdom progression. This is particularly important because we will never successfully change mindsets that we don't identify as being a problem in the first place.

Furthermore, we will never change what we can tolerate. In order for an individual to change anything he or she must be tired of the repeated cycles of defeat, of the consequences of that particular thought, action or way. To put it in the vernacular, we must become sick and tired of being sick and tired.

The question must follow: Are you willing to do what it takes to achieve success in that area?

This is also an incredibly important question. It might seem like the answer would be obvious, but each person's answer is not always what you'd think. Once we know our direction, and we've committed to seeing it through, we can move on to step two.

2. PRAYER

Next we begin to pray about the problem. Prayer serves many functions. Prayer releases things to God, but it's also a means to receive things from Him. Prayer becomes an outlet for all of the clutter that has been clogging up our hearts and minds. When we pray, we are able to lay all of our problems, situations and circumstances before the Lord. The Word of God says, "Cast all of your cares upon Him, for He careth for you," (I Peter 5:7).

Through prayer, God will allow you to cast your cares upon Him and in return He begins to download into your spirit your specific ingredients for change. He will begin to pour out His love, and you will truly experience the Savior for yourself. He will also give you greater levels of revelation regarding your particular issue. At the same time you will begin to trust the Lord. When you trust God you will also trust His Word – both what He impresses upon your heart and what is written in the bible.

3. LEARN THE RELEVANT 'AFTER CHRIST' INFORMATION

Once you know where you would like to have a greater degree of success and you've asked God about it, do a *Word Search*. Find out what the bible says about that subject. Do a contextual word study on it (use a concordance to find each place it's mentioned in scripture and read those and their surrounding passages). Saturate yourself in the Word of God. You will begin to learn what God's heart is on the matter. God's Word is a lamp unto our feet and a light unto our path (Psalm 119:105). It is able to give you insight in a situation and lead you into each step He wants you to take. Listen to your pastor's teachings on it. Pastors have been placed into your life to feed you with knowledge and understanding. Visit a Christian bookstore. Look through the shelves and find prominent authors on the subject. You may want to make an investment and buy some good Christian literature. You can also search online. There are incredibly vast resources available in this country on the bible and biblical doctrine. We must be resourceful and relentless in our pursuit of change.

We can also draw from each others' testimonies (Revelation 12:11). We are people with kindred problems. We don't have to always discover solutions on our own. We can borrow revelation through what others have received from the Lord. Their testimony can help facilitate your breakthrough. Once we begin to learn how others have overcome, it helps us overcome.

It is important that your research and theory come from a reliable source. It should come from sources and people in whom you have confidence.

Once you have an idea of what the bible has to say about the subject, consult your pastor or spiritual mentor for additional insight. Take notes on what you learn. Develop an outline of what

CHAPTER SEVEN: **STEPS FOR CHANGE**

you've discovered. You want to make sure that you aren't missing anything important.

> "Study to show thy self approved, a workman that need not be ashamed, rightly dividing the Word of truth."
>
> — II Timothy 2:15

Please don't underestimate the importance of this research. If we proceed to the next stage without making sure our "new" system of thinking is biblically accurate and applicable, then we can be trading one erroneous self-destructive mindset for another that is just as dangerous.

Once you've learned your new perspective, take it into your prayer closet. It's time to renew the subconscious.

4. MEDITATION

As our passages in Joshua and Psalms showed us, meditation is crucial to changing our system of thinking. It will not only help you change your system of thinking but it will facilitate your success economically, socially, emotionally and so on.

Meditation allows us to relax in the presence of

the Lord. It gives an opportunity for God to speak to us unhindered. Meditation is essential because it facilitates revelation from God for the answers we are seeking. It needs to be a part of our prayer life because it demands that we be quiet in God's presence allowing Him to speak. Many of us dump all of our problems on God in prayer and then hang up the line. But we must understand that God meets us in prayer. We must give Him a chance to speak. When He speaks through meditation it seeps and settles into the heart thereby cultivating change.

Whatever we practice becomes a practice;

Once the Word becomes a part of our subconscious, it becomes second nature for us to draw upon it. Therefore, when it comes time to make a decision, we have immediate access to the Word rather than just drawing upon our old processed thought patterns.

When studying your bible, you don't always have to read chapters. Just read a verse and meditate on it. Rehearse this verse in your heart and in your mouth. Try to commit some verses to memory.

When we do this we begin to process the Word into our hearts. It becomes a part of who you are. Now, when the old man's arguments come to you, you have an arsenal against him. We can proclaim the Word as Jesus did.

5. PRACTICE NEW HABITS

Once we have revelation about what the bible says, we must put our faith in action. Practice, practice, practice. Once we begin to practice our new habits, we retrain ourselves. At this point you begin to tell your subconscious that you are serious about change and it will make a mental note of it. **Whatever we practice becomes a practice;** meaning, it becomes a part of our lives. If you practice sin, then sin becomes a practice in your life. But if you practice godliness, then godliness becomes a practice in your life. Sometimes you have to do it, even when you don't feel like doing it because you're still fighting against old mindsets. But the longer you work at it, the easier it becomes.

— *Food for Thought* —

1. In what area(s) of life would you like to have more success?

2. Are you willing to do what it takes to have success in those areas?

3. Do you have a prayer partner or anyone you trust who can keep you accountable to follow these steps?

4. Are you ready to experience success in your life like never before?

Chapter Eight
THE RESULTS OF RENEWING YOUR MIND

Over the years I've found that a lot of Christians tend to look around and believe that everyone else is prospering, growing and moving forward faster than they are. We often think we're not moving fast enough based on some erroneous comparison (II Corinthians 10:12) or erroneous assumption of what things are supposed to look like given to us by our old man. The truth is that it's all in our system of thinking.

That person who is successful is successful because they have the right system of thinking to achieve success in that area of their life. It's a process. How you process information is going to determine what you have in life from the tangible to the intangible.

So the challenge now rests with us. The

gauntlet has been thrown. Will we choose to renew our minds; to cast off that self-destructive old man and take on the position of undeniably successful purpose-fulfilling Kingdom-minded sons of God?

He promised it to you if you'll obey.

I challenge you. Renew your mind. I guarantee, the rewards are greater than you could possibly imagine.

Acknowledgements

To my Lord and Savior Jesus Christ who is absolutely the source and strength of my life. Without You this book would not be possible. It's All About You!

To Pastors Bob Atkins, Carlos Keith and Chris Jordan thanks for being spiritual fathers and mentors. Your belief in the call of God upon my life is continuously affirming. Thanks for the unconditional love.

To the saints of Kingdom Life Empowerment Center Church, I love you and appreciate the caliber of people you are. Thanks for your faithfulness and support of the vision.

Special thanks to Sister Ebony Burke for transcribing my sermons. Without your initial work on this book it would not be in print today.

Special thanks also to Minister Darlean French for your touch of brilliance.

Thanks to Minister Stephen Blackmon, Consuming Fire Inc and Kingdom Rule Publishing. You all are superb!

Last but not least. Thanks to my parents Henry Thomas Wells Sr. and Shirley Ann Wells. I appreciate all you have done to help make me the person that I am today. I love you both!

About the Author

PASTOR HENRY T. WELLS is the Senior Pastor of Kingdom Life Empowerment Center Church of Williamsburg. He is a visionary leader who God has gifted with both prophetic and practical insights needed to strengthen the Body of Christ.

Pastor Wells is a caring and compassionate leader, who believes that living by example is the best policy for a man's life. He is committed to God and to the advancement of His Kingdom. He is known for being transparent and uncompromising

Pastor Wells is a 13-year veteran of the U.S. Army where he served in U.S. Army Chaplaincy Corps. He is currently employed by the Department of Army (Civil Service) as a Business Advisor for one its Contracting Agencies. He holds both an Associates degree in Liberal Arts (2001) and a

Bachelor of Arts degree in Business Administration (2003), Saint Leo University. He is currently pursuing two Masters Degrees in Theology and Business.

He is married to the former Donyale Denise Johnson who serves as CoPastor. They are proud parents of two sons Henry and Josiah.

For additional copies of

RENEWING YOUR MIND
THE KEY TO UNDENIABLE SUCCESS

Please write:

Kingdom Life Empowerment Center Church
438 McLaws Circle
Williamsburg, VA 23185

Call:
(757) 220-5655

Email:
pastor@klecc.org
Or visit us online at
www.klecc.org
or
www.kingdomrule.com

www.ingramcontent.com/pod-product-compliance
Lightning Source LLC
LaVergne TN
LVHW051154080426
835508LV00021B/2625